If They Can Do It, We Can Too!

Kids Write About Famous People Who Overcame Learning Differences Similar to Theirs

by the students from Deephaven School's Learning Lab
and their teacher, Margo Holen Dinneen

DEACONESS PRESS
Minneapolis, Minnesota

ISBN 0-925190-61-6
Library of Congress Catalog Card Number 92-072157

First Printing: November 1992

Printed in the United States of America
96 95 94 93 92   7 6 5 4 3 2 1

Cover design by Susan Kroese

Publisher's Note: Deaconess Press publishes books and pamphlets related to the subjects of physical health, mental health, and chemical dependency. Its publications, including *If They Can Do It, We Can Too!*, do not necessarily reflect the philosophy of Fairview or Fairview Deaconess, or its treatment programs.

Dedication

This book is dedicated with love to Kenny Allen, who died in a boating accident shortly after completion of the original version of this book. Kenny was a very special friend to all of us, and he left our lives much too soon. We all miss him.

"I remember that Kenny would try to break up scuffles. He was really determined when he set his mind to something. If you knew Kenny, he was really nice. He was tough on the outside but really nice on the inside. He was warm to people who knew him."
—Kirk Miller

"Kenny had lots of freckles, kind of a long face, and straight real light brown hair. He really liked hockey and boats. He was really funny. He always liked to make people laugh."
—Chris Bloomer

"Kenny was in my class in fourth grade. He liked to kid around—to tell jokes and stuff. He was happy all the time."
—Matt Patterson

"Kenny gave everyone he touched many very special memories, and I am no exception. I feel blessed to have known him."
—Margo Holen Dinneen

Acknowledgments

The first edition of this book, like the one you are now reading, was authored by Learning Lab students from transition (between kindergarten and first grade) to fourth grade. There is no way it could have been produced in eleven weeks without the help of the following people:

Sources: A sincere thank you to John Hyre, Mary Bernt, and Barb Lewis, who brought boxes of information for the students from five local school and public libraries. The students and their parents, friends, and relatives brought in valuable information too, creating a nine page resource list and sharing the materials equally among all the young contributors. P.J.'s Aunt Holly deserves thanks for assisting the kids in corresponding with several celebrities.

Production: Our production crew included parents and grandparents who sat for endless hours with the students, reading with them, helping some of them write down what they wanted to say, binding books, and doing so many other tasks too numerous to name. Lee Allison copied and typed, Deb Markham lent computer expertise, Susan Kroese designed the covers for both editions, and Al and Pam Scott helped with lettering, printing, and collating. My team teacher, Mikki Krueger, and my prayer partner, Laury Baars, helped teach. Margery Martin and Fran Richter wrote out invoices and mailed out books.

Cheering Us On: Those who supported us included Don Draayer, National Superintendent of the Year; Bev Montgomery, Minnetonka Special Ed Director; Brad Board, Deephaven Principal; and Judi Mollerus, Minnetonka Public Relations Director. Also, thanks to Barb Vogt and all the wonderful Deephaven teachers who endured all the commotion, and to Jeanne Molzahn, who took hundreds of messages. In addition to her production help, Margery Martin planned two celebrations which were enjoyed by both the students and their parents.

Promotion: Our publicity team was unsolicited. Thanks to WCCO TV News, which featured the kids in two stories, and Paragon Educational Cable TV, which produced a 53 minute broadcast. Also, thanks to Muriel Rossman, from the Arizona Department of Education, and Jacque Wuertenberg, Nationwide Teacher Trainer from St. Louis, Missouri. Both Muriel and Jacque have broadened our horizons.

Contractual Administration: With all the parties involved, the negotiations necessary to bring this book to its present publication were complex. Ed Wedman, Editor-in-Chief of Deaconess Press, Tom Berge, Business Director of Minnetonka Schools, and Bob Kroese, parent advocate, managed to design a contract upon which eighteen families, one publisher, and a school district could agree. They have our thanks, as does former Minnesota Attorney General Miles Lord, a local resident, for volunteering his legal expertise.

Publication: The credit for bringing out this new Deaconess Press edition of *If They Can Do It, We Can Too!* must first go to the students, for their work and patience. The input and encouragement of the parents was also invaluable. Susan Kroese deserves special thanks for contributing her piece, entitled "A Parent's Perspective," and for designing this cover. Finally, it was Jack Caravela, Deaconess Press Senior Editor, who weeded through four years of documentation to produce this book!

To My Students: You teach me as much every day as I teach you! Can you imagine what it's like to learn about 18 famous adults and 18 soon-to-be-famous students all at once? I am so proud when, one by one, you come to me saying, "Margo, I don't think I need you anymore!" You have accomplished so much in the time that we've worked together, and I hope you will always remember never to settle for less than the best you can do.

Good luck!

Love,
Margo
☺

Table of Contents

Introduction

Deephaven Elementary School is nestled in the wonderful school district of Minnetonka, Minnesota. It is a National School of Excellence Finalist and serves about 400 neighborhood children in kindergarten to fourth grade.

Early in my life I knew that I wanted to teach kids who needed extra help in school, and I've spent 27 years as a teacher doing just that. The last twelve of those years have been in the Deephaven Learning Lab, where I teach many different subjects and skills to students who learn in different ways. Some of them come into my room for half of each school day. Others come in for one or more short sessions each day. Still others just check in whenever they need a little extra help. I love what I do and I love all the students I work with, so I can't imagine a better job in the whole world!

On September 28, 1988, three third grade boys named Tom Rawitzer, Peter Richter, and Andy Wrase came into the Learning Lab ready to work. Tom gave me a puzzled look and asked, "Margo, can we write a book this year?"

"Sure," I replied. "What do you want to write about?"

Peter said, "Well, you tell us we're really smart." And Andy said, "You say there are lots of famous people with learning differences. Can we write about them?"

That was the beginning of the most exciting and fun project of my teaching career!

I thought that the idea might appeal to my other students, so I made a list of famous people with learning differences from a file of readings and quotes I'd collected. I included people who were challenged by learning to read and write, people who needed extra help with speech and language, and even a few people who are left-handed. (Perhaps I should mention that being a lefty is also a learning difference that can require some extra attention.)

Within a couple of days, 18 of my students had each chosen a hero to research and write about. They all had wonderful reasons for choosing the people they did!

Immediately they started to bring in books, baseball cards, posters, and other materials to help each other with their reports. It was so wonderful to see how every student became interested in the celebrities that the other kids were writing about as well as their own heroes. I sat totally amazed one day listening to a first grader who was just learning to read (Will Martin) explain to another beginning reader (Matthew Kroese) all about Leonardo da Vinci from a *National Geographic* magazine he brought to share. Researching the chapters was a real team effort!

The second week of the project, first grader Shawn Svoboda was concentrating on copying over part of his chapter. Under his breath he muttered, "If they can do it, we can too!" At that moment I knew we had a title for our book!

Soon some of the students began making drawings and cutting out magazine photos to paste into the book. They also started coming up with suggestions for the book's format. One asked, "Can we autograph the books?" Another suggested sequencing the chapters by order of the earliest birthdate (Leonardo da Vinci, 1452) to the most recent (Tom Cruise, 1962). With some quick subtraction, you'll notice that the famous people profiled in our book span 510 years of history!

In case I haven't made it clear already, this project was the kids' idea, and I was merely an assistant. Some days I could barely keep up with them, they were so determined to write *their* book.

Our Superintendent, Dr. Donald Draayer (recently named National School Superintendent of the Year), made an impromptu visit to our classroom one day and learned about our project. In November of 1988 he featured our project in the *Minnetonka School News,* a newsletter which is mailed to all district taxpayers. This recognition both motivated the students and held them accountable to do their very best.

Only once did I question the wisdom of the project. Was it too complex for the younger children? Would it meet legal educational goals? As soon as I began to list the things that my students were learning, I had no more doubts. They included:

1. The students learned teamwork and the value of helping each other.

2. They learned to be responsible about bringing in things they found for themselves or promised for others.

3. They learned to ask questions of their teachers, parents, other relatives, and neighbors.

4. They learned to use the school library and the public library and caught radio and television news briefs.

5. They had to listen and read carefully as they absorbed volumes of information from many different sources.

6. They organized that information and put it into their own words.

7. They learned about spacing, margins, and indenting as well as careful cutting, pasting, and copying. Some had the courage to try cursive writing.

8. They learned correct capitalization and

punctuation rules, such as where to use periods, commas, hyphens, quotation marks, and question marks, and they learned to underline titles.

9. They spelled very difficult words.

10. They gained a better understanding of learning differences and a healthy respect for both their own talents and the areas that needed improvement.

11. They wrote thank you notes to every single person who helped them.

12. Twelve of them wrote letters and addressed envelopes to their famous people, or to historical foundations.

13. They learned to be good sports when others got mail and they didn't.

14. Their confidence soared as their self-esteem grew!

Our school district agreed to print 100 copies of our book. Andrew and Matthew Kroese's mother volunteered to design the cover, and their father became an advocate for the project. He talked to our school district about putting the profits from book sales into a trust fund for Deephaven Learning Lab students.

Our next milestone was on Friday, January 6, 1989, when a Minneapolis television station (WCCO) featured the students on both their 6:00 p.m. and 10:00 p.m. news programs! The news reporter and cameraman who covered the story spent almost two hours in our Learning Lab, interviewing and filming the completion of our book! We all felt proud when the lead-in on the news that evening was read: "Local and international news this week is so depressing that WCCO is thrilled to bring you some Minnetonka students with their message of hope."

After the television report aired we were flooded with phone requests for the book from all over the Midwest. (Through the efforts of parents and teachers, copies of the book have now been shared in Canada, the British Isles, Germany, and U.S. states from coast to coast.) One of the calls that came in the very next day was from Deaconess Press, telling us that they would like to professionally publish the book. The students were very excited. Their project would be available in schools and bookstores across the country!

In May of 1991, the eight youngest kids still at Deephaven Elementary were videotaped reading their chapters for a local cable television station (Paragon Educational Cable TV). The resulting program was shown four times.

At the time of this book's publication, only one student of the eighteen will still be at Deephaven. But the fellowship, bonding, teamwork, and love built through this project will last a lifetime for these kids, their families, and me.

While the typeset book you are reading neatly reproduces the students' essays in their own words, it can't reflect their tremendous struggles to sequence words and sentences correctly and to write them frontwards and right side up on a line. This alone was an amazing feat for primary grade kids with special needs!

In case it doesn't show, I am proud of these students. They picked about the most challenging project in the world for them to do, and they did their very best! I congratulate each and every one of them!

I hope that the students who read this book will think about the kids who wrote it and say to themselves, "if they can do it, we can too!"

Margo

Margo Holen Dinneen

"Success is to be measured not so much by the position that one has reached in life as by the obstacles which he has overcome while trying to succeed."

—Booker T. Washington

Matthew Kroese

Matthew Kroese is a twin who was born prematurely and weighed only eighteen ounces at the age of three weeks! To me he is a miracle!

Matthew was in 1st grade when he wrote his chapter for this book. Just before writing it he told me that he wanted to be an artist and inventor someday, so it was a natural choice for him to write about Leonardo da Vinci.

Matthew's handwriting is beautiful. Reading, spelling, and oral language have been especially challenging to him, but he works very hard and learns best through hearing.

Matthew loves swimming, soccer, and Cub Scouts, and is active in his church. He and his family do much public service for children in our inner city and around the world.

Matthew's brother Andrew wrote the story about Michael Landon on page 41.

I decided to write about Leonardo da Vinci. He is famous as an Artist. I want to be an artist Someday.

Leonardo da Vinci

by Matthew Kroese, age 8 years, 2 months

I decided to write about Leonardo da Vinci. He is famous as an artist. I want to be an artist someday.

He was born on April 15, 1452, in Vinci, Italy. His dad was a lawyer named Ser Piero da Vinci. His mom was a peasant girl named Catarina but they weren't married. Later his dad got married to someone else.

Leonardo had blue eyes and really blond hair. He was curious about everything and he loved nature. Leonardo liked drawing horses and riding horses. He collected wasps, lizards, and bats. He was an excellent musician.

Leonardo was a better painter than his teacher. He was better than the other kids at almost everything. A problem, though. He didn't finish his work. He changed his mind, and he got bored. Reading, writing, and paying attention were hard. When Leonardo couldn't think of the words he drew the pictures.

Leonardo worked for Andrea del Verrocchio for six years when he was a teenager. They made jewelry and painted pictures for churches. At the same time he also studied architecture, geometry, and engineering. Leonardo was left-handed.

When Leonardo was 20 in 1472 he joined the guild of painters so he could earn money. But he didn't earn any for six years.

During the years 1478 to 1482, Leonardo had his own studio and painted a famous painting called *The Adoration of the Three Kings*. Leonardo did at least 10,000 drawings that are now in art museums around the world. His most famous painting is the *Mona Lisa*. It is cracked and faded now, but at first it showed every eyelash.

Leonardo liked to invent stuff. He loved to learn everything. He liked to draw knots and put them in his pictures. He was a genius and his artwork is some of the best in the world. He never got married but he liked women.

Leonardo was a famous artist and sculptor. He was an inventor, an architect, a writer, an engineer, a musician, and other things.

Leonardo da Vinci was an unhappy man when he died on May 2, 1519. He couldn't finish the work he had started.

I liked writing about Leonardo da Vinci because it is the first chapter in the book. It was fun!

Afterword

Matthew has made great progress since writing this chapter because he has worked so hard all year round. He now is in 5th grade at Minnetonka Intermediate School, and while he is still working on improving his reading, he regularly gets perfect scores on his spelling, math, and geography tests. Matthew is a beautiful skier, snowboarder, and dancer. The violin is a new interest, and he plays very well. He is a perfectionist, and while he will always do his best, he is leaning to work more quickly.

An unforgettable memory for me was when Matthew and Andrew took me out to dinner at a very nice restaurant, all dressed up in suits and ties (they were in first grade at the time). They insisted that they wanted to do this themselves, without their parents. (Mrs. Kroese joined us for dessert.) I had a wonderful time in the company of these two young gentlemen.

Will Martin

Will Martin was just starting first grade when we began to write this book, and he truly bubbled over with enthusiasm!

Will wanted to write about a U.S. President, and chose James Garfield from the list of famous people I'd put up. Almost daily he brought in resource material for his own chapter and for many other students as well. Will was knowledgeable about a broad range of subjects and loved to discuss them. He was a gentle and caring person who was a good role model for other kids.

While Will was always excellent at reading, spelling, and math, he needed to work on his organization skills and handwriting. Working on this book was great practice for him, and I'm sure that his interest in computers will serve him well in the future.

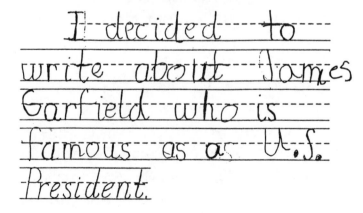

I decided to write about James Garfield who is famous as a U.S. President.

James Garfield
by Will Martin, age 7

I decided to write about James Garfield who is famous as a U.S. President. I like the Garfield cartoon and I am interested in Presidents.

He was born on November 19, 1831, in Orange, Ohio. His name then was James Abram Garfield. His parents were Abram, a farmer, and Eliza. His dad died before he was two years old. His two brothers and two sisters were older than him. They belonged to Disciples of Christ Church.

In school he was a lefty. When he was young he pulled barges with a horse.

James went to Williams College in Williamstown, Massachusetts. He graduated on August 6, 1856. When he was almost 27 years old he married Lucretia who he had played with when he was little. Later she was his student. They had seven children.

James was six feet tall and had big shoulders. His face was round with a beard that was long and heavy.

It was hard being left handed. He wrote one language with one hand and at the same time another language with his other hand.

In the Civil War he commanded soldiers. He had never been a soldier before, but he looked it up in books. He was so good that after the war he got elected to Congress. He was elected President in 1880.

A killer shot him in 1881 because he wanted the Vice President to become President. Garfield was 49 when he died. He will be remembered as a very famous President of the United States.

There are at least 11 places in the U.S.A. named after him. I want to be famous too.

Afterword

Will is now in 5th grade at Minnetonka Intermediate school. When I asked his mother for an update on what he is doing now, she told me that Will insisted on editing her comments and typing the following paragraph himself on a computer:

"Will Martin, now 10 years old, describes himself as funny, athletic, adventurous, and happy. He says, 'I enjoy gym and social studies. In my free time, I like snowboarding, skiing, soccer, hockey, and football.'"

Will remains interested in James Garfield. During the project he learned about a mountain named Garfield, and found out that his parents had climbed it. This led to a search for other places named Garfield, and he drew a map of the United States naming 11 places which were named after this former President.

Way to go, Will!

Tom Rawitzer

Tom Rawitzer was one of the three 3rd grade boys who came up with the idea to write this book. He knew right away that he wanted to write about Thomas Edison.

Attention and focus were difficult for Tom, and somehow I felt that he wished spelling and handwriting had never been invented! But Tom had great ideas, was very good in math, and through hard work became a good reader. Tom is a goalie for his hockey team, and he is a good one! He also loves skiing and playing golf.

Tom worked hard at learning to share feelings in a healthy way. I still have a cartoon that Tom drew. It is a picture of a clown lying on a bed. He is saying, "It is hard work trying to keep people happy and laughing. Clowns need a rest."

I decided to write about Thomas Alva Edison who is famous as the Inventor of the electric light because my name is Thomas Alvin Rawitzer.

Thomas Alva Edison

by Tom Rawitzer, age 9 years, 10 months

I decided to write about **Thomas Alva** Edison, who is famous as the inventor of the electric light, because my name is **Thomas Alvin** Rawitzer.

He was born on February 11, 1847, in Ohio. His parents were Nancy and Samuel. They were rich when he was born. Thomas was the youngest of seven children, but three of them died before he was born.

In school his teacher, Rev. G. B. Engle, called him "addled," a dreamer. He said he asked too many questions. He had scarlet fever at age 7 and it left him hard of hearing.

Tom's mom realized he needed special education. She took him out of school and started teaching him herself. He began reading many books and especially liked *The School of Natural Philosophy* by R.G. Parker about scientific experiments he could do at home. In his basement Tom loved experimenting so much that he wanted to skip meals. As a little boy, Tom worked on the railroad from 7:00 in the morning to 9:00 at night. He sold candy, newspapers and magazines. Tom never missed a chance to earn money.

When he was 13 he asked the train man if he could build a laboratory in the baggage car. But when he was 15, some of his chemicals spilled and the baggage car caught fire. The laboratory got tossed off the train. Al also had burned down his dad's barn when he was a little boy just to see what a fire would do.

Before Al knew his ABCs he was copying store signs on his slate. When he was ten, he read college level books.

One time Al wanted to see if he could hatch

eggs like chickens do. He sat on eggs for hours in a neighbor's barn. Most of the eggs were on the seat of his pants!

Thomas was fascinated by electricity and he really liked the telegraph. In fact he even proposed to his wife by tapping his message in Morse code. They were religious.

He was happy because he had his wife, Mary Stillwell, and his laboratory. They had three children. She died 13 years later. Tom got married again two years later to Nina Miller and they had two more children. Both marriages were failures because he worked too much. One of his sons, Charles, was Governor of New Jersey from 1941 to 1944.

Thomas was the world's greatest inventor. Every country in the world has honored him. He patented over 1300 inventions in 60 years. It was called "The Age of Edison."

Edison worked such long hours that he took naps at his desk with books for pillows. He whistled, sang, and laughed while he worked.

Thomas always studied by experiment. He never gave up on an idea. One time he made 10,000 experiments with one storage battery. He didn't think he failed. He just found 10,000 ways it didn't work.

Edison was called a genius. He said, "Genius is 1% inspiration and 99% perspiration."

Some of Edison's most famous inventions are the electric light, phonograph, motion picture, stock ticker tape, voting machine, electric power station, cement mixer, copy machines, and many other things.

By old age he was so deaf he could only hear a shout. Thomas could have had surgery but he refused. He died on 10/18/31 in New Jersey at age 84. 29 years later Edison was elected to the Great American Hall of Fame. His laboratory was made a National Monument and Milan, Ohio was restored as his birthplace. President Eisenhower declared a proclamation that said: "When he was honored by other governments, he said the honor was not for him but for his country." The inscription on the Congressional Medal of Honor stated, "He illuminated the path of progress by his inventions."

I learned a lot by writing this report. Thomas Edison never gave up. He really challenged me to keep on trying.

Afterword

After our book was finished, Tom sent a copy to the Edison National Historic Site, where Thomas Edison's laboratories still stand. He was delighted when he received a letter from Park Ranger Gregory F. Smith, thanking him for the book and telling him that it had been put in a very special place in the park library.

Tom is now in the 7th Grade at Minnetonka Junior High School. His hobbies are rollerblading, skateboarding, skiing, golf, football and baseball.

His mom reports that as a result of working on the book, Tom now thinks of Thomas Edison as a real person who had a tremendous attitude about the challenges he faced. Tom also learned that he could express his ideas in an interesting way, and this increased his confidence in himself.

Peter Richter

Peter Richter is one of three boys in his family. His brother Jesse wrote the chapter on George Patton.

Peter didn't have the benefit of an extra academic year in the early grades, as many kids with L.D. do. He was easily distracted, had some speech and language needs, and also had to overcome mild asthma and vision problems. When he was in the 1st grade, reading seemed almost impossible to him, but he had a great attitude. He would work at his goals until he mastered them, and he became a good student. He was one of the boys who came to me with the idea for this book.

Peter developed beautiful handwriting, and when a local TV station did a story on our book, he did a fine job of reading his chapter on the air. He also loved to ski and was a good baseball player.

I decided to write about Albert Einstein who is famous as an American physicist because he didn't seem smart when he was young but he got really smart and I liked him.

Albert Einstein

by Peter Richter, age 9 1/2

I decided to write about Albert Einstein who is famous as an American physicist because he didn't seem smart when he was young but he got really smart and I liked him.

He was born March 14, 1879, in Ulm, Germany. His parents were Hermann, who had an electrical business, and his mom's name was Pauline. Albert was their only son. They were Jewish.

He was slow in learning to talk. He did not start until age 4, and even at age 9, his speech was not fluent. His parents feared he might be retarded.

He disliked sports and games, but he loved mechanical toys and figuring out how they worked. Especially a compass given to him by his dad when he was sick. He was a rebellious, stubborn student and disliked all authority.

In 1895, his dad's business failed and his family moved to Milan, Italy, but Albert stayed behind in Munich at a boarding school. He disliked it so much he got a doctor to write him a note saying he was on the edge of a nervous breakdown. He said he should have a leave of absence, but when he got to school he discovered they had already expelled him for being unruly and insulting. He called his teachers "sergeants" in grade school and "lieutenants" in high school.

Albert flunked math and barely passed chemistry and geometry. He had trouble learning French.

Science was his life's work. Time and space were important to him. He taught himself calculus and higher mathematics. Albert did very well at college physics before he was eleven. He was a good violin player and was great in Latin and Greek. When Albert was 16 he went to technical school in Italy. He was supposed to be 18 and he failed the test.

Albert went to a school in Italy for one year. Then he tried the test again. This time he passed and he started at the Federal Institute of Technology.

Kids in school sometimes called Albert "Mr. Dullard" because he was dyslexic and had a hard time reading but he did very well in science and became the world's greatest scientist.

Einstein got his first job as a teacher in a technical institute. Then in 1902 he began work in the Swiss Patent Office. While working there, he got his Ph.D. degree and started working on his theory of relativity. He became so famous for his theory that he was made director of the Kaiser Wilhelm Institute in Germany and a member of the Prussian Academy of Sciences. This gave him more time to do his research.

In 1921, Einstein got the Nobel Prize in physics.

In 1928, he had a heart attack from over-work and had to quit his job.

In 1933, Einstein decided to leave Germany because Hitler was persecuting Jews. He came to Princeton, New Jersey, to the Institute for Advanced Study.

Dr. Einstein's wife, Elsa, who was his cousin, died in 1936. He was also married to Mileria Marck for 15 years and had two sons, Albert Jr. and Edward. The following years he devoted to science. In September, 1939, he wrote a letter to President Roosevelt about atomic warfare.

Einstein wrote many scientific books during his lifetime. Many of them dealt with Relativity and his Unified Field Theory. In 1955, at the age of 76, Einstein died.

He was truly a very famous, brilliant man, even though he had several learning problems as a child.

I am glad I had an opportunity to learn about him.

Afterword

Shortly after we finished our book, a class of 2nd graders at another school read it and wrote to tell us how much they liked it. Peter wrote back to thank them for their letters and said that he had lots of fun writing about Albert Einstein.

Peter is now in the 7th grade, and has just started attending Minnetonka Junior High. His mother told me that working on his chapter helped him to learn how to organize his facts and ideas, and that he now uses these skills when he writes reports for school. He no longer needs help with his learning differences, and has really come a long way!

Peter enjoys skiing, baseball and football. (I was lucky one Saturday to catch all three Richters playing their separate baseball games.) Peter also plays the clarinet and has a pet chinchilla named Cuddles.

Jesse Richter

Jesse Richter was in a grade we call Transition, between kindergarten and 1st grade, when he wrote this chapter. He was the youngest student to work on this book, but his enthusiasm was equal to any of the others. With the help of his mom and other adults, Jesse learned many things about General Patton. He then explained what he wanted to say, and the adults wrote it down. For the final draft, Jesse insisted on writing the words he could read in his own handwriting (227). I wrote the others (112). He also surprised me one day with a twelve page booklet of his own drawings showing scenes of World War II.

Reading and vocabulary were areas where Jesse had to work extra hard, and he was also overcoming the effects of a hearing impairment. Jesse is a math whiz, and he enjoys skiing and football. His brother Peter wrote the chapter on Albert Einstein.

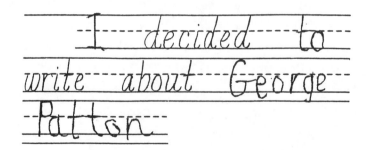

I decided to write about George Patton

George Patton

by Jesse Richter, age 6 years, 10 months

I decided to write about George Patton, who was famous as an American Army General, because I like G.I. Joes and my Grandpa was in the army.

He was born on November 11, 1885, in San Gabriel, California. His name then was George Smith Patton. His parents were ranchers.

In school he was a bad student. He could not read even at age 12 because he had a learning disability. He had a good brain and he could write. The kids teased him a lot.

George was a great sailor. He couldn't read but he could sail across the ocean. He liked sports. He was in the Olympics and won in running, horseback riding, swimming, and target shooting. He used his good brain and memory to get through West Point in five years. He could repeat everything word for word, but had trouble with math which made him have to go for an extra year. He wrote two books and gave good speeches.

On May 26, 1910, at age 25, he married Beatrice Ayer. She was the daughter of a Boston businessman that owned the American Woolen Company. Beatrice was a writer. They had two daughters and one son.

The Pattons liked to sail. They wanted to sail around the world on their 60 foot sailboat called the *When and If*. They also had a farmhouse at Hamilton, Massachusetts, where Mrs. Patton and the children stayed when General Patton was off to war. He would come and be with them for a little while.

George Patton had told his wife that he would die in the war. But instead he was killed in a car accident on December 21, 1945 at age 60.

When he was leading the army, he made

our new Tank-Borne Cavalry. In 1916 he was assigned to Pershing's staff at the head of the American Expeditionary Force. His Army nickname was "Old Blood and Guts." He was awarded a Distinguished Service Medal that said, "By his energy and sound judgment he rendered very valuable services in his organization and direction of the tank center at the Army Schools at Langres. In the employment of the Tank Corps troops in combat he displayed high military attainments, zeal, and marked adaptability in a form of warfare comparatively new to the American Army."

We had a 103rd birthday party for George Patton. I liked writing about him.

Afterword

Jesse is now in 4th grade, and he is doing quite well in school. Not only is math still a strong subject for him, but he is also becoming a very good speller, and his handwriting is excellent. His mother reports that while he is still interested in art and drawing, since he wrote his chapter he has started to take karate lessons. He recently achieved the rank of brown belt. He has also taken an interest in the trampoline, and can now do both front and back flips.

When a local cable television station came to our school to do a report on the creation of this book, Jesse was one of the students who read his chapter on the air. His mother tells me that he found it challenging to work on this book, especially since he was not yet in first grade, and that he learned a lot from the experience.

Brad Sampson

Although schoolwork has never been easy for Brad, he is one of the hardest workers I have ever known. In spite of the challenges he faced in researching and writing his chapter on Babe Ruth, he was the first student to finish his chapter for our earlier edition.

Brad has Attention Deficit Disorder, which means that concentrating in class is especially difficult for him. Organization is a challenge, too. Fortunately, he is able to take a medication which helps him a great deal. Two real strengths for Brad are remembering information that he hears and the ability to draw well.

No teacher could ask for a more devoted student than Brad. He is a wonderful peer tutor for younger students who have learning differences, and is a great example to them. He likes baseball, football, snowboarding, and skiing, and he really thrives on helping others.

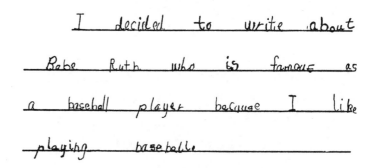

I decided to write about Babe Ruth who is famous as a baseball player because I like playing baseball.

Babe Ruth

by Brad Sampson, age 7 years, 10 months

I decided to write about Babe Ruth who is famous as a baseball player because I like playing baseball.

He was born on February 6, 1895, in Baltimore, Maryland. His name then was George Herman Ehrhardt. His parents were a waterfront worker and a country girl. They were very poor and he didn't know where the next meal was coming from, but he didn't care.

He was a big black haired 7 year old. In school he got in too much trouble and he was sent away to a Catholic school. He got in too many fights. At 18 he still was getting into trouble, like for skipping school to go fishing.

While he was growing up he loved to pitch but he didn't care about slugging. George was a lefty.

Coach Jack Dunn from the Baltimore Orioles came to the Catholic school to watch him pitch. That day he asked George to sign a contract and asked to be his guardian. The team said, "Well, here's Jack's newest babe now!" And his name changed to Babe Ruth!

At age 19 he married a 16 year old waitress from Texas named Helen Woodford, but he thought he was 20 years old. They had two babies but they died. Later they took care of a girl named Dorothy.

When he got rich, he gambled and drank too much. The Mayor asked Babe Ruth to stop doing bad things for the kids' sake. They were at a big dinner in New York. Babe Ruth cried when he promised to shape up. And he kept his promise. He never got in trouble again.

One day a child, Johnny Sylvester, was dying in a hospital. Babe came and said "I'll hit a home run for you!" And he did!

After Babe Ruth and Helen separated, she died in a fire. In 1929 he married Claire Hodgson. They adopted Dorothy and Claire's daughter Julia.

He was 6'2" and weighed 215 pounds and he was pigeon-toed.

Babe Ruth was a pitcher and outfielder for the Boston Red Sox. Then he went to the New York Yankees and hit 714 home runs. That was a world's record. He struck out 1330 times too. That's a world's record too, but I guess he just kept on trying.

When he quit baseball he played golf and bowled to lose weight. I like to golf and bowl, too. He wrote two booklets about how to play baseball. He visited army men during the war and Catholic groups for free.

Babe Ruth didn't like growing old. He died on August 16, 1948, in New York. Yankee Stadium is still called "The House that Ruth Built."

Extra! Extra! Read all about it! I just learned that when Babe Ruth was little he lived upstairs from his dad's bar. His parents beat him up. When he was 7, Babe ran wild on the streets and chewed tobacco and drank whiskey. Then he was sent away to St. Mary's Industrial School for Boys. His mom died in a fire and his dad was murdered in a fight.

He was in love with the game of baseball. When he was 18, Baltimore offered him $600.00 a season. He said he would have played for nothing because he loved the game so much. Babe was the king of home runs. He made 61 baseball records, including 28 in the World Series.

On August 16, 1948, he died of cancer. It was very sad.

If Babe Ruth could become famous, I can too! I want to play baseball like him.

Afterword

After we finished working on this book, Brad Sampson participated in the program that a cable television station did on us. During a panel discussion with some of the other students, Brad said, "I can't believe how many people didn't give up, and I can't believe that they let us publish this book."

Brad is now in 5th grade at Minnetonka Intermediate School. He continues to be very interested in sports, and his friends are very important to him.

Brad's parents tell me that he is still interested in Babe Ruth, and that whenever he hears about the other celebrities who are included in this book, he rarely fails to mention what he remembers about them. When he's having a hard time with schoolwork, he often finds encouragement by recalling the role models in this book and telling himself, "if they can do it, so can I."

Elizabeth Nelson

I vividly remember the day when third grader Elizabeth **Nelson** looked at the long list of celebrities' names and said, "Well, I can only read one word ("Nelson"), so I guess I'll write about him!" Like **Nelson** Rockefeller and a number of other famous people in this book, Elizabeth could not sound out words and learn to read in the way that many people do. (Having an attention deficit disorder was also a challenge for her.) There are other ways to learn, however, and if Elizabeth keeps working hard and gets the help she needs, she will succeed at whatever she decides to do.

Elizabeth is very smart, creative, and friendly. Math was easy for her, and she enjoyed skiing, sailing, swimming, soccer, and football. I can envision her becoming a champion skier, swimmer, or gymnast someday, and her mother thinks she might become the president of a corporation!

I chose to write about Nelson Rockefeller who was famous as a vice president of the United States because he has my name.

Nelson Rockefeller

by Elizabeth Nelson, age 8 years, 11 months

I chose to write about Nelson Rockefeller who was famous as a Vice President of the United States because he has my name.

He was born on 7/8/08 in New York. His name then was Nelson Aldrich Rockefeller.

Nelson Rockefeller's grandpa, John D. Rockefeller, Sr., started Standard Oil Company and gave away a lot of money. He also started the University of Chicago. Nelson Rockefeller's father, John D. Rockefeller, Jr., took over the handling of family money and founded Rockefeller Center, which is 14 buildings, including a 70 story skyscraper. Nelson's mother, Abby Greene Aldrich, in 1929 helped found the New York Museum of Modern Art.

Nelson Rockefeller, who was five feet ten and a half inches in height, had blue-grey eyes, and light brown hair. He was called husky and handsome.

He went to Dartmouth College where his favorite sports were soccer and skiing. He taught Sunday school, edited the college magazine and was elected Phi Beta Kappa. He graduated cum laude.

He married Mary Clark. He got married on June 30, 1930. On their honeymoon they went around the world. The names of their five children are Rodmen, Steven, Ann, and the twins, Michael and Mary. His second wife was called Happy.

Nelson Rockefeller's first job was as a clerk at the Chase National Bank. In the afternoons he worked in the rental center of the Rockefeller Center. In 1958 he was elected Governor of New York. He had top government positions under Presidents Roosevelt, Truman, and Eisenhower. President Ford nominated

Nelson Rockefeller to be Vice President. The Democratic Congress confirmed him in December 1974 and he took office.

Nelson Rockefeller wasn't always famous. He thought it was very hard in school. He was left-handed and had a learning difference. I am glad I wasn't him.

He had dyslexia. He once said, "I struggled to understand words that seemed to garble before my eyes, numbers that came out backwards, sentences which were hard to grasp."

I learned a lot about Nelson Rockefeller's family and about him. Even though he had a learning difference, he still became a Vice President of the U.S.A. Even though I have L.D., I can be the greatest photographer or veterinarian!

Afterword

Elizabeth was the first student to write a letter to the subject of his or her chapter. Nelson Rockefeller died in 1979, but a woman at Rockefeller Plaza who answers questions about the former Vice President wrote back. Elizabeth was very excited to receive the letter, and when we finished the first version of this book, she sent a copy to the woman. She asked that it either be sent to a relative of Nelson Rockefeller or kept in Rockefeller Center.

Shortly after this book was written, Elizabeth moved to Rapid City, South Dakota, but I've seen her eight or ten times since then when she has visited Minnetonka. Now in 7th grade, Elizabeth is interested in music as well as sports. She is in the Rapid City Children's Choir, plays the flute, and is taking piano lessons. Last year she was in her grade's top math group and took first place in the girls' long jump.

Chris Bloomer

Chris Bloomer knew right away that he wanted to write about his famous uncle, former President Gerald Ford. He was fortunate enough to receive information from the person who was the subject of his chapter, and President Ford was a great source of encouragement to Chris throughout the project.

I remember Chris as a warm, patient, and friendly person who expressed himself very well in words. Reading was more difficult, because he had a tendency to reverse the order of words and letters, and like many people, being left-handed made handwriting more challenging. But Chris soon learned that these obstacles could be overcome, and he has made tremendous progress.

At the time when he was writing his chapter, Chris was involved in Cub Scouts and enjoyed soccer, skiing, swimming, and golf.

I chose to write about Gerald Ford who is famous as the 38th President of the USA because he is my dad's aunts husband

Gerald Ford

by Chris Bloomer, age 10 1/2

I chose to write about Gerald Ford, who is famous as the 38th President of the U.S.A., because he is my dad's aunt's husband.

He was born on July 14, 1913, in Omaha, Nebraska. His name then was Leslie King, Jr. His parents were Leslie and Dorothy, but they soon divorced and his mother married Gerald Ford, who gave him his name. They were middle class. His half brothers were Thomas, Richard, and James.

When Gerald Ford was five the doctor took out his appendix and discovered after the surgery that they did not need to take his appendix out.

At 8 or 9 he had a stuttering problem. At 10 the problem went away. As he grew older he ate with his left hand and played golf right-handed.

When Gerald was in high school, his real father stopped to see him at the restaurant where he worked. That was the first time he had seen his father since he was a baby.

In school he was a star football player and a very good student. He was named all-city and all-state center because he was a star on his team, the Trojans. Gerald was also an Eagle Scout.

He went to the University of Michigan and then to Yale University. Two of his favorite subjects were history and government.

A year after he became a lawyer he joined the Navy because of the attack on Pearl Harbor by the Japanese. He sailed on the aircraft carrier *Monterey* in the Pacific.

On October 15, 1948, at age 35, he married Elizabeth Bloomer, who was a fashion coordinator for a department store and a dancer.

They had four children: Michael, John, Steven, and Susan.

Gerald Ford then served as a Congressman from Michigan for the next twenty-five years. He then became Vice President and served with Richard Nixon. When Nixon resigned, Vice President Ford became President of the U.S.A. Ford pardoned Richard Nixon even though it may have cost him the future Presidency. He picked Nelson Rockefeller to be his Vice President.

There have been two attempts on his life. The first was in September, 1975, in California. He noticed a woman walking through the crowd like she wanted to shake his hand. When he put out his hand to shake her hand she pulled out a gun. President Ford ducked and the secret service brought her down and Ford into the Capitol.

The second attempt happened a couple of weeks later. He was getting into his car to go to the airport. He heard a big bang. The secret service pushed him into the floor of the car and drove away as fast as possible.

President Ford currently lives with his wife Betty in California. He also spends time in Vail, Colorado. I hope to meet him someday.

While I have been working on this report, I realized that not all successful people have easy lives. Even though some people have a hard time, that doesn't mean thay can't be anything that they want to be.

President Ford will be remembered as being an honest and hardworking man.

Afterword

Chris had written to President Ford and received a letter, photograph, and other research materials. Later he sent a finished book, and President Ford responded with a letter saying: "Congratulations on the excellent report on my life. I am honored you selected me for your report." Chris got to meet his famous uncle in person when he and his family visited the Fords that Christmas in Colorado.

His parents wrote to tell me that Chris still enjoys skiing and soccer, is on a swim team, and likes tennis and golf. He collects and swaps trading cards as a hobby.

Chris keeps in touch with President Ford about once a year and continues to draw inspiration from his uncle. He is now in 8th grade in Wayzata, Minnesota and is doing very well in school. Chris has learned to live with his learning difference and rarely needs any special help with schoolwork.

Andrew Kroese

I've often wondered if Andrew Kroese and his brother (who wrote the chapter about Leonardo da Vinci) are really identical twins. Andrew learns by watching and works quickly to get to the next task; Matthew learns by hearing and works slowly to make sure everything is correct.

Andrew has always loved to draw and is very creative. He needs visual clues to remember what he learns and to organize his work, but by giving his best effort, he has made wonderful progress. His handwriting is excellent, and he enjoyed many activities in 1st grade, including baseball, jazz and tap dancing, skating, and swimming.

This chapter was written before Michael Landon died of cancer in 1991, and Andrew was very sad when he heard the news. Like so many of the students who worked on this book, Andrew felt a special connection to the person he wrote about.

41

I decided to write about Michael Landon who is famous as a Tv actor because I like the book Little House On the prairie.

Michael Landon

by Andrew Kroese, age 8 years, 2 months

I decided to write about Michael Landon, who is famous as a tv actor, because I like the book *Little House on the Prairie*.

He was born on October 31, 1936 or 1937, in New York. His name then was Eugene Maurice Orowitz. His parents were Eli Orowitz, a publicist, and Peggy O'Neill, an actress. He had one sister who changed her name to Victoria King when she became an actress.

Eugene and another boy had to stay after school and clean the blackboard and erasers. They were Jewish, and the other kids got out early to go to church. He wet his bed until he was a teenager. He was a famous javelin thrower. People were surprised that he was a good javelin thrower because he was so small. Eugene almost didn't make it through high school because he practiced the javelin so much. He also worked in a local soup factory.

When Eugene was 17 he got a track scholarship to the University of Southern California. The next year he dropped out.

Then he went to Warner Brothers Acting School. He looked in the phone book and changed his name to Michael Landon. His first movie was *I Was a Teenage Werewolf*. When he was 22 Michael was Little Joe on "Bonanza." He was on the show for 13 years. It was about cowboys.

Then he was Dad on "Little House on the Prairie" for years. 40,000 kids named "Little House on the Prairie" as their favorite. At first Michael did not want to do "Little House on the Prairie." Then he decided he did, because his 12 year old girl liked it.

They wanted "Little House" to really seem real so they looked at every old photograph they could find. Every building is exactly like real old buildings.

He has green eyes, brown curly hair, he's 5'11" tall. He likes to play golf. He likes to make Texas chili. He had eight kids. He got married three times. Michael Landon fights against drugs. He goes to a club to work out every day.

Michael is a good actor and director and writer but he wanted everything to be too perfect. Then he argued a lot. But he admits his mistakes and says, "If Michael Landon bombs, I don't want anyone else to have to take the blame but Michael Landon."

In 1973, Michael Landon sang and danced on a special variety show. He was also on the Johnny Carson show.

He wrote and directed a story called "The Wish." It was about a man named Hoss, who made friends with a black family. It was Michael Landon's favorite.

He is a guardian angel on "Highway to Heaven" now. Michael works 16 hours a day.

Michael earns $665,113 per month. He is rich. His house in Beverly Hills cost $10 million. It has 13 bathrooms, a library, a movie room, and a "Bonanza" room with everything from that tv show. It even has the outhouse.

I liked writing about Michael Landon. I liked putting the writing and pictures together.

Afterword

Andrew is now in 5th grade at Minnetonka Intermediate School. His reading, spelling, and math have all improved a lot, and he has needed less help with his studies every year.

Both Andrew and his brother have benefitted so much from the support and encouragement that their mother and father give to them. The entire Kroese family has done everything they could to help with this book, and all the work that Susan and Bob Kroese have taken on (including working with our publisher, Deaconess Press) is not only greatly appreciated by me, but also by all the student authors. Andrew and Matthew know that they have a super mom and dad.

Andrew enjoys soccer, skiing, Cub Scouts, playing the saxophone, and public service, and as he grows up, I know that his natural talent for making new friends will serve him well.

Jaime Keefer

Although Jaime Keefer told me that she found most television shows boring and would even rather do homework than watch them, she did like television star Henry Winkler, and wanted to write about him.

Jaime was in 1st grade when she wrote her chapter. She was a quiet girl who liked to read and write, and she had great motivation to work hard.

Of all the students, Jaime was probably the one who had the least amount of help to write her chapter. Although she and the other students shared information whenever they found some on another person's topic, she was very independent when it came to choosing what to write and putting it down on paper.

Jaime appeared on the cable tv program that did a show on us, and did a fine job of reading her chapter on the air.

Henry Winkler was born on October 30, 1945 He was raised in a strict Jewish home.

Henry Winkler
by Jaime Keefer, age 8

Henry Winkler was born on October 30, 1945. He was raised in a strict Jewish home. Henry had a sister named Beatrice. He was very shy and was often teased by his classmates. Sometimes he cried himself to sleep. Henry is proud to be Jewish. His dad was president of a lumber company.

Henry went to a boys' school in New York. Henry had learning differences, but he studied a lot. He went to a private school in Switzerland, too.

Henry is 5 feet 6 1/2 inches tall and weighs about 140 pounds. He plays music and talks to his plants. He smokes cigarettes but not when he's working. Henry really didn't like motorcycles. He thinks drinkers get sickeningly drunk. Henry doesn't like to be crowded, only with a few people.

At first he was scared to interview, but when they believed in him he felt ten feet tall. He was afraid he'd never get any fan mail. Now he gets 9 out of every 10 letters to Paramount Movie Studio.

He earned $30,000 a week.

In 1973, Henry Winkler started being "The Fonz" on "Happy Days." Fonzarelli is a made up character who dropped out of high school because he couldn't read. Henry is ten years older than Fonzie. Fonz says "Ayyyy" with his thumbs up. Henry felt that "there was a lot more to Fonzie than just being cool. There were plenty of good things going for him and I wanted to explore them."

Henry was wondering if being Fonzie was doing anybody any good. Then there was a little girl who was autistic. She came to see Fonzie at the music center. Her first word at age 5 was "Fonzie." That was a miracle!

Henry Winkler graduated from Emerson College in drama where he learned to be an actor. Then he got a masters degree in drama at Yale University. At first he practiced his acting on television commercials for toothpaste and airlines and pizza.

Fonzie was so famous that his jacket is in the Smithsonian Institute.

There are at least 100 companies that made "Fonz" things like socks, posters, puzzles, bubble gum, and dolls.

Henry was married in 1978 to Stacey Weitzman. They have two children. Zoe Emily is 8 years old and Max is 5. Henry has dark brown hair and hazel eyes. They live in California. He makes $1.1 million a year.

Henry likes to work in his rock garden and to read Shakespeare.

Henry loves kids and he does lots of volunteer work for kids. He helps LD kids at Glendale Grade School. He works for Toys for Tots and the Epilepsy Foundation. Henry helps to give dying children their last big wish through the Starlight Foundation. He also runs a Special Arts Festival for handicapped kids in California.

It felt good to write this book about Henry Winkler. I am glad that he's so nice to kids!

Afterword

Jaime is now in 5th grade in Minnetonka and has made so much progress that she no longer needs any special academic help. She is an excellent speller, she is good in math, and her handwriting is beautiful. She still loves to read, and also likes to go fishing and camping with her family.

After we finished the first version of this book, Jaime sent it to Henry Winkler along with a letter telling him that she had fun writing it and hoped he would enjoy it. So far she hasn't received a reply from Mr. Winkler, but maybe he will write back if he sees this new version of our book.

Jaime recently wrote about her feelings about working on this book. She wrote:

"Writing the book made me feel great! At first I wasn't sure if I could do it or not, but after I got started I didn't want to stop!"

Tracy Fuller

Tracy Fuller was in 3rd grade when she wrote her chapter about Cher. She was a quiet, pleasant person who was very athletic and who loved animals. Reading and math were difficult for her, but she has worked hard and has improved quite a bit in both areas. Tracy was always a good speller and writer.

While we were writing this book, Tracy helped more students with their chapters than anyone else. She was always looking for information, and brought some in for eleven different students.

Tracy has been very involved with church activities and enjoys swimming, diving, and gymnastics. She also is a Girl Scout, takes piano lessons, and babysits three times a week! I wish I had as much energy as she does!

I wanted to write about Cher Bono who is famous as a movie star and singer because I like to watch movies.

Cher

by Tracy Fuller, age 9 years, 2 months

I wanted to write about Cher, who is famous as a movie star and a singer because I like to watch movies. She was born on May 20, 1946 in California. Her name then was Cherilyn Sarkesian Lapierre.

Her parents were Georgia and Gilbert. Her mom was a fashion model who married eight times. Georgia married Cher's dad three times but he was a heroin addict who was in jail all the time. Her dad was a bank manager. They were rich and poor and rich and poor all the time. They moved all the time. Cher went to some public schools, a private school, and a Catholic charity home. She had a sister Georgeanne. They grew up in Los Angeles, California. When Cher was little she had to wrap rubber bands around her shoes to keep the bottoms on.

Cher is part Indian, part Armenian, part Turkish, and part French. When she was five she wanted to become famous.

Cher had trouble in school and dropped out in 11th grade. Then she studied drama. A year later she married Salvatore "Sonny" Bono when she was 18 and he was 28 or 29. Their parents thought they were too young to get married so they ran away to Mexico on October 27, 1964.

They were married for 11 years. Their daughter Chastity was born in 1969 when Cher was 25.

When they were divorced she still didn't know how to write a check. Really Cher didn't know that she had LD until she was 30. A doctor tested Chastity when she was 7 years old because she was doing so badly in school.

Cher still has trouble reading cue cards for

songs and movies. Cher got married again for two years in 1975 to Gregg Allman. He also was a drug addict and they had a boy named Elijah Blue. Eight days after she and Gregg were married Cher filed for divorce. She stayed with him for 2 1/2 more years while he tried to quit drinking and drugs but he couldn't. Gregg has only seen Elijah four times since 1977.

Cher's teenage nickname was "Pinky." In 1965, Sonny and Cher borrowed $168 to record their first hit song "Baby Don't Go" but they called themselves Caesar and Cleo then.

Then they recorded "I Got You, Babe," "Bang Bang," and "The Beat Goes On," which made them really famous.

Now Cher is making movies and she almost took home an Academy Award in 1983. Her movies are:

1982: *Come Back to the 5 and Dime, Jimmy Dean, Jimmy Dean*
1983: *Silkwood*
1985: *Mask*
1987: *The Witches of Eastwick*
1987: *Suspect*
1987: *Moonstruck*

Cher always had a good sense of humor but some of it was very cutting. "I thought it best to have a big mouth so that people would be afraid to mess with you than to let everyone come up and tap dance on your head."

Cher enjoys wearing strange outfits on TV in order to get attention.

She has a booming voice and her eyes are open really wide.

When she was 41 Cher learned to be tough. She won't let anyone tell her what to do anymore.

Cher wants everything to be perfect and sometimes she gets stubborn and difficult. I like things to be perfect too but I don't get stubborn.

Cher has always fought against drugs. Sonny and Cher made a movie about marijuana that the U.S. Government gave to high schools.

I have L.D. and so does Cher. I enjoy watching tv but I like writing about her better.

Afterword

Tracy sent a copy of our book and a letter to Cher, and she was one of the lucky students who received a personal reply. I'll never forget the look in her eyes when she told me, "I got a letter from Cher today!"

Cher wrote Tracy a two page, handwritten letter that told her how much she liked the chapter that Tracy wrote and how she wished that there had been a book like this one when she was a girl. Cher also wrote about how difficult school was for her. This letter was very inspiring to Tracy, and I'm sure that she will treasure it forever.

Tracy is now in 7th grade and continues to work hard at her studies. She is still quite an athlete, and before she left Deephaven School she broke the all-time school record for the girls' one mile run!

Shawn Svoboda

Shawn Svoboda was in 1st grade when he wrote his chapter on Mark Spitz. He is the student who gave this book its name. He was copying his chapter, writing and erasing to get everything just right, when he said to himself, "If they can do it, I can too!"

Shawn is a very handsome and active guy who had to work extra hard because reading, writing, math, and following directions were all challenging to him. His organization skills are good, though, and when he recognizes the things he has to work on, Shawn makes steady progress. I'm proud of him.

Shawn picked Mark Spitz from my list of lefties because he liked to swim. He also enjoyed biking, skiing, and Cub Scouts, and I remember how important it was to him when his mother came into school one day to help him with his chapter.

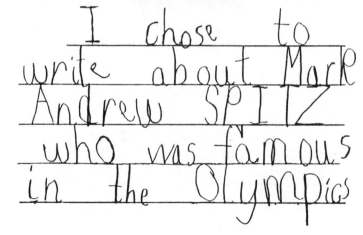

I chose to write about Mark Andrew SPITZ who was famous in the Olympics

53

Mark Spitz

by Shawn Svoboda, age 7 1/2

I chose to write about Mark Andrew Spitz who was famous in the Olympics because I like good swimmers.

He was born on February 10, 1950, in California. He had two younger sisters, Heidi and Nancy who liked to swim too. When Mark was two years old he started swimming.

His family moved to Hawaii for two years and he swam every day. Then he moved back to California. His dad would ask "How many win?" and Mark would answer "One." Mark's dad pushed because he was great at swimming.

Their dad pushed him because winning was everything to him.

Mark Spitz started swimming lessons when he was eight years old, but he already knew how to swim. He was a gifted swimmer and so their family got a coach. His name was Sherman Chavoor.

When Mark was ten he held seven national age group records. He was practicing one and one half hours every day.

Mark's father really pushed him. His father got him excused from Hebrew lessons so he could practice. He told the rabbi "Even God likes a winner." His dad would ask him, "How many lanes in the pool?" and Mark would say "Six."

Mark Spitz graduated from Santa Clara High School in California in June 1968. Mark wanted to be a dentist and a swimmer, so he picked the University of Indiana because they had a good swim team and a dental program.

Mark liked winning, but sometimes he was sad because he didn't have many friends. The other swimmers felt jealous because Mark won all the time. Sometimes Mark had trouble getting along with his coach too.

Mark married Susan Weiner who was a model. Susan's and Mark's dads are friends. Their dream is to live in a big house on the ocean in California. Suzy and Mark have a son Matt who is 7 like me.

I like writing about Mark Spitz because I want to grow up like him.

Afterword

While researching his chapter, Shawn wrote a letter to Mark Spitz and waited weeks to mail it until P.J. Bernt's mom finally found the address for a clothing store that Mark Spitz owns. Later Shawn sent a book and another letter there. He was very excited when he received an autograph and note, which read: "To Shawn Svoboda, my good friend. Nice Work. Mark Spitz."

During the next school year, in a video-taped discussion about the book, Shawn asked, "Will I really be able to buy one in a bookstore?"

A special triumph for Shawn was when he read his chapter on cable tv, because two of the things he had worked so hard to improve were speech and reading. He did a good job!

Shawn is now in 5th grade, and I encourage him to stay positive and keep trying his very best.

Kenny Allen

Kenny Allen was a bright 4th grade student who had lots of energy and was willing to work hard to reach his organization and social goals. We had a hamster in my classroom, and students who earned enough points for positive academics and behavior got to take it home on weekends and vacations. I remember how Kenny worked for months, finally earning 300 points to take the hamster home for a few days.

Kenny chose to write about his favorite musician. Stevie Wonder's learning difference is his blindness, and the way he overcame this disability was very inspiring to Kenny. Kenny wrote to Stevie Wonder when he started his chapter and was very pleased and excited when he received an autographed photo and some information from the Stevie Wonder Fan Club.

Kenny loved his family, church, sailing, and hockey.

I asked to write about Stevie Wonder, who is famous as a blind singer and pianist, because I like his music.

Stevie Wonder

by Kenny Allen, age 9 years, 8 months

I asked to write about Stevie Wonder, who is famous as a blind singer and pianist, because I like his music.

He was born on May 13th, 1950, in Saginaw, Michigan. His name then was Stevland Judkins Morris. His mother's name was Lula Mae and his stepdad was Paul Hardaway. He was a baker. They were very very poor. Stevie Wonder has three brothers and two sisters.

It was unbelieveable that Stevland was alive. He was born four weeks early and lived in an incubator for a month. They pumped too much oxygen into the incubator and he got growths behind his eyeballs. That made him blind. Now he has a dislocated nerve in one eye and a cataract in the other.

Like any normal kid, he climbed trees, rode a bike, and fooled around. By age two he pounded a tin pan with a spoon to the music on the radio. When he was four he could play piano and a harmonica his uncle gave him. He played toy drums, and when he broke them all, a men's club gave him a real set for Christmas.

His first stage was the steps of a neighborhood building. By eight years old, he was lead singer of a church but he got kicked out for playing rock and roll with his friends.

When Stevie was nine years old, a friend's brother brought him to Motown. He hung around there after school and people called him "little boy wonder." In 1963 he made his first record, and he was named "Little Stevie Wonder." It was called "Finger Tips II" and it was a real hit around the world. It sold 1,000,000 copies and was his first gold record.

Stevie earned lots of money which was put into a trust account until he was 21, but he only earned an allowance of $2.50 per week. The court appointed Motown to be his guardian.

Stevie's dad never paid attention to him. A man at Motown, Clarence Paul, sort of adopted him and was like his dad.

At first Stevie went to a public school, then he went to a school for the blind. When he travelled he had a private tutor. He graduated from the Michigan School for the Blind when he was 19.

At the age of 21, Stevie's music career began to grow and he became more creative, writing his own music. In 1974 at age 24 Stevie sold over 40,000,000 copies of Wonder records.

Stevie Wonder uses no drugs, although the way he moves his head back and forth has been mistaken for a drug "high." He has explained that his head movements are "blindisens." Blindisens are an energy release through the eyes of a blind person.

Stevie has won many awards during his career. He won 14 Grammys from 1974-1977 and also 3 album of the year awards. In 1988 Stevie began to produce videos.

In addition to his music, Stevie Wonder is a great humanitarian. He was involved in helping to push the U.S. Congress into declaring Martin Luther King Day a national holiday. Wonder was an important player in 1985's "We Are the World." Millions of dollars were raised to feed the starving Africans.

With Stevie's busy schedule he still finds time to be a successful businessman and loving father to daughter Aisha. Stevie wrote "Isn't She Lovely" after her. Stevie Wonder is a world-known singer, songwriter, producer, humanitarian and an incredible person.

In writing this report, I have learned that

with hard work, handicapped people can do anything normal people can do.

Afterword

Kenny Allen died in a boating accident on June 28, 1989, when he was ten years old. All of us who knew Kenny still miss him, and we will never forget his enthusiasm or how he always gave his best effort to reach any goal he set for himself. A good example of this quality is the fact that Kenny wasn't even a daily student in my class when he wrote his chapter on Stevie Wonder. He did all his work in his own free time at school and at home with his parents because he wanted to be part of the project.

On the day we heard that Kenny had died I saw five of the other students who wrote chapters for this book. All of them asked me if we could dedicate this book to Kenny, and the other authors felt the same way.

Once again, we dedicate this book to you, Kenny! We miss you.

Aubrey Rahn

3rd grader Aubrey Rahn decided that she wanted to write about a woman celebrity. A friend of hers told her about Ann Bancroft, the only woman who had ever traveled by dog sled to the North Pole. Shortly after this, Aubrey went with her dad and sister to hear Ann Bancroft give a presentation at a local college. She wrote and received many letters to Ann and other contacts, and was very enthusiastic about writing a chapter on her!

Aubrey has always been a good reader and speller and had fine handwriting, but math was a challenge for her. She also had to work hard to overcome her shyness in groups. Aubrey has done a good job, and in primary school even became interested in being an actress when she grows up! Some of her favorite activities have included the YMCA Leadership Camp and putting on neighborhood plays with her friends.

Ann was born in Minnesota on 9-29-55. She grew up in St. Paul with two brothers and two sisters.

Ann Bancroft

by Aubrey Rahn, age 9 years, 9 months

Ann was born in Minnesota on 9-29-55. She grew up in St. Paul with two brothers and two sisters. From first grade on, she was tutored or in special classes because she had a lot of trouble learning in school. She had dyslexia. Ann writes and eats with her left hand but she bats and golfs with her right hand.

Ann grew up on Sunfish Lake with her mom and dad, Dick and Debbie. Her brothers were Hunter and Bill and her sisters were Sarah and Carrie. They all camped together. Ann went to Summit Elementary Girls School. Then she went to St. Paul Academy Junior High School. There she was with boys and girls. She graduated from Sibley Public High School.

Ann was great in sports. She loved tennis and basketball and was a camp counselor.

Ann went to the University of Wyoming for a few years. She graduated from the University of Oregon with a Bachelor of Science degree in Physical Education. Ann was a Phy. Ed. teacher for Barton Elementary School in Minneapolis. She also taught physical education to handicapped kids and taught rock climbing, backpacking, canoeing, and cross-country skiing.

Ann still lives in St.Paul near where she grew up. She is 33 years old now and is 5 feet 3 inches tall. She has brown hair and brown eyes that twinkle when she laughs.

In August 1979, Ann went with 8 other people to Alaska. They hiked in the Brooks Range—the Gate of Arctic National Monument.

Ann was the 2nd oldest of the five children. She was too busy to be in the band or be a cheerleader. A friend of mine said that Ann and her family went to the House of Hope Presbyterian Church in St. Paul when she was growing up. Her family went on long backpacking and white water canoeing trips and went mountain climbing.

Ann heard about an expedition to the North Pole and wanted to go. She was one of the candidates for the trip, but was told she couldn't go because she was a woman. But Will Steger, who was the leader, called Ann the next day and told her she could go.

Ann quit her job as a teacher so she could prepare for the journey. It took three years of training, eight people, 75 dogs, and ten months of hard training in Canada. They made their own clothes and food and equipment to take on the trip.

Ann had a very important part on the expedition. She was in charge of all the dogs and the photography. The other members of the expedition were Will, who is from Ely, Minnesota, the co-leader, Paul, also from Ely, Bob, from New Zealand, Richard, from Onebee, Canada (Richard was a skier scout), Jeff, from Wyoming, Brent, from Canada, and Bob, from Chicago. Forty-nine of the seventy-five dogs went on the trip. These were the best trained dogs. They planned the trip to leave in March and be gone until May. The reason for going at this time was because it was before summer and the snow melt.

I went to hear Ann Bancroft talk. This is what she said. They flew for ten hours in a big plane with no heat because it would get too hot for the dogs. Then they flew in six small planes.

When it was 30 degrees below zero the tents still were warm. The sleeping bags weighed 12 pounds but when they got cold and damp they weighed 50 pounds. There were 3 people to a sleeping bag. They slept like spoons with one in the middle.

The five sleds were pulled by dog teams. They weighed 1400 pounds and were too heavy for people so Ann and the men walked alongside.

They ate oatmeal with no sugar or milk, just a stick of butter. At noon they had hot tea, but no lunch. Their dinner was 70% fat—dry beef, cheese, and butter. This was 5,000 to 8,000 calories per day. They had to eat fast because the food would freeze and get hard.

They all worked 18 hours a day and they couldn't get wet because their clothes would never get dry. Ann had only one change of clothes.

Two of the men had to quit the trip because one hurt his leg and the other froze his toes until they turned black.

On May 1, 1986, Ann and the five men reached the North Pole. They had been dog sledding for 55 days and went about a thousand miles. Sometimes it got to be 70 degrees below zero. Four of the six of them were left handed.

Ann gave the speech when they got to the North Pole. She said "It is a great day for us. We thank God we've arrived at the top of the world in good health and spirits. We are deeply indebted to the forty-nine huskies and Canadian Eskimo dogs who pulled so long and hard to bring us here. They are the real heroes of this journey.

"The journey across the polar sea was filled with paradox. Surrounded by the gentle pastel beauty of the ice, snow, and low-lying sun, we endured the hardest work and most hostile conditions any of us have ever experienced. At times there were tears of despair when obstacle after obstacle seemed to spell defeat. At times we were overwhelmed by exhilaration as we made major breakthroughs.

"But most of the time we just worked hard, wrestling every mile of forward progress from the sea ice. We experienced pain, cold, hunger, and fatigue. For us, the significance of this is that we are able to better empathize with people all over the world for whom these are daily experiences much of their lives, and who deserve the world's attention more than we do.

"Our only regret is that two of our team members, Bob Mantell and Bob McKerrow, who gave everything they had for this journey before injury turned them back, are not here to share this moment with us. To them, we dedicate this day."

Since the trip, she has been writing a book and getting lots of awards. Read about them.

Since her return from the Pole, Ann has been featured in national magazines like "People," "In Fashion," "McCalls," "Vogue," "UltraSport," and "Ms." She has been lauded as "Ms. Woman of the Year," "Regina High School Woman of the Year," and "Twin Citian of the Year" (by *Twin Cities* Magazine), as well as receiving awards of achievement from the March of Dimes, Melpomene Institute, the Lab School of Washington, the Children's Museum of Indianapolis, Groves School, and the Y.W.C.A. of Minneapolis.

"She currently speaks to national and international groups, is writing a book about her expedition experiences, and in addition is working as a staff member with Wilderness Inquiry II."

It has been really, really exciting writing about Ann Bancroft! I loved having her come to my school to be on tv with me!

Afterword

Aubrey wrote to Ann Bancroft and told her about the book that she and the other students were writing. She invited Ann to come to our school to help her with the book, and the day that Ann arrived, WCCO TV News broadcasted their story on us! Meeting Ann Bancroft meant so much to Aubrey, and Aubrey continues to follow Ann's projects and accomplishments through the newpaper and television.

Now in Junior High in St. Paul, Aubrey no longer needs any special help in school. In fact, last year she was in the top math group in her class! Her mother tells me that she has made so many new friends and is so busy with a variety of activities that it is hard to believe she was ever shy! Aubrey is on the School Patrol and still wants to be a professional actress.

P.J. Bernt

P.J. Bernt was in 3rd Grade when he wrote his chapter. He didn't find John Elway on the list of famous people I had prepared, but since John Elway was his hero and had been trained to bat left-handed, it was decided that P.J. could write about him.

P.J. was always good at reading and math, but handwriting and organization were very difficult for him. Much of his writing turned out backwards, upside down, or on top of itself. P.J's hard work and determination brought steady improvement, and his careful handwriting when he wrote out his chapter showed what good work he learned to do.

I remember P.J. being very interested in nature and conservation, and that he liked animals. He raised chinchillas and other pets, was a good soccer player, and was very involved in his church and Cub Scouts.

I asked to write about John Elway who is famous as a Denver Bronco foot ball player because I used to live in Denver and he's my favorite quarter back.

John Elway

by P.J. Bernt, age 9 years, 7 months

I asked to write about John Elway who is famous as a Denver Bronco football player because I used to live in Denver and he's my favorite quarterback.

John was born on June 28, 1960 in Port Angeles, Washington. His Dad was Jack, a basketball and football coach. He had two sisters. One was a twin who he competed with for everything, even taking out the garbage and getting good grades.

When he was only two years old, he picked up a plastic baseball bat in the living room. He swung right handed, but his dad said "No, no, no, that's not the way you should do it. Left handed hitters have an advantage in baseball." Today John still hits left handed but he's right handed for everything else.

John knew he had to practice everything. He liked to throw the football around with his dad. In 5th grade John started being a running back because he was the fastest runner in his class. When John got bigger in 7th grade he lost his speed and he became a quarterback. John knew for sure he was going to be a football player as well as a quarterback when he started high school. John went to the summer camp at Washington State from 6th to 9th grade.

John always practiced throwing the football with his receivers in the spring and summer, 300 or 400 times a day. John couldn't jump well and he couldn't dunk a basketball.

After 9th grade, John's family moved to a suburb of Los Angeles, California from Washington. Here he graduated from Granada Hills High School which had a strong football program. He got good grades and he said "I always felt that I was better than someone who was doing drugs. I never wanted to be lowered to their level."

John graduated with a major in Economics from Stanford University in 1983. Baltimore tried to recruit him but he said, "I would rather play minor league baseball than pro football in Baltimore."

John has blond hair and blue eyes and a wonderful smile. He is 6' 3" tall and weighs 215 pounds. John's wife is Janet who also went to Stanford and graduated in sociology. She is tall and athletic. They live in Aurora, Colorado, and their daughter Jessica is blonde and blue eyed. John's favorite food is strawberry angel food cake. They have a Ford Bronco and a Jaguar. He likes to play cards, fish, and golf. When Jessica was 14 months old John and Janet were expecting another baby.

Denver traded for Elway in 1983. Coach Dan Reeves asked him right away to lift weights but John didn't want to. Roger Staubach called and talked him into it. Now John can bench 300-350 pounds.

Elway says "the best advice my mom and dad ever gave me was to treat other people the way you wish to be treated." John Elway is famous for his strong arm, and he is the most highly paid quarterback in the NFL. He earns 5 million dollars a year. Did you know that Elway also played college baseball and he was drafted by the New York Yankees for their minor league team?

I want to be a nice person like John Elway. It would be great if I could play football like him too!

Afterword

P.J. wrote to John Elway in care of the Denver Broncos Football Team. He received a packet of biographical information about his hero, and he was very excited to get it.

It turned out that in addition to his learning difference, there was something else that made school harder for P.J. He had allergies to milk and to a certain artificial sweetener. When it was learned that he would feel better if he didn't have these things, he started to avoid them. P.J. was able to do much better in class when he stayed away from the foods that caused problems for him.

P.J. moved to California before he started 6th grade, and he is in 7th grade now in Custer, South Dakota. His mother tells me he is doing well with his studies, that he still loves animals, and that he continues to be very interested in nature.

Andy Wrase

Andy Wrase was one of the 3rd graders who came to me with the idea of writing this book. It was a real challenge for Andy to complete his chapter on Greg Louganis. Although he had good ideas and could read well orally, Andy had difficulty forming his thoughts into complete sentences and paragraphs. He also had some trouble with his spelling, but that began to improve once he started to wear glasses. A very significant day for Andy was when his mom came to school to help him with his chapter.

Andy asked for extra tutoring so he could make faster progress in his schoolwork. Nothing could stop him when he made up his mind to learn something.

At the time he wrote his chapter, Andy was learning to ski and enjoyed playing soccer and basketball. He also participated in Cub Scouts.

Greg Efthimios was born in Samoa in 1960. He was adopted by Peter and Frances Louganis.

Greg Louganis

by Andy Wrase, age 8 years, 10 months

Greg Efthimios was born in Samoa in 1960. He was adopted by Peter and Francis Louganis. When he was little he was teased because of his dark skin.

Greg's older sister, Despina, was also adopted. They lived near San Diego, California. When they were two or three, they started taking dance lessons. When he went to school he was teased because he had a reading disability. Then Greg spent all of his free time in the gym, where he danced.

When Greg was little he had asthma. The doctor told him he should have more exercise, so he started gymnastics, too. Then he practiced tumbling off the diving board into the swimming pool. That's when Greg started taking diving lessons.

When Greg was eighteen he found out he had learning differences. Also, his legs were bow-legged a little bit. When he's diving he sees the water between his legs. After high school he graduated from U.C. Irvine in Drama. He wanted to be an actor.

Greg is five feet nine inches tall and weighs between 150 and 168 pounds. He is shy and has a quiet voice. Greg likes to be alone or with close friends. He doesn't like crowds. When Greg was taking dance lessons he learned how to really concentrate.

Greg quit smoking and drinking to set a good example for kids. When he quit, his diving got much better. I saw him on a T.V. ad. He said, "Don't Smoke. Diving is more fun!" It *is* fun! Greg was in the Junior Olympics in 1971 in Colorado. He scored a perfect ten on his diving.

In 1976 he got a silver medal at the Olympics when he was only sixteen years old. He was the first diver to earn a perfect score from all seven judges in an international competition. Greg practices diving every day. He makes 75-100 dives a day.

Greg doesn't like to lift weights at an exercise club. He loves dancing and diving instead. Greg has made 180,000 springboard dives in his 18 year career. He's the best diver in history. But Greg never had an easy time in school. His life seemed terrible back then.

I want to be like Greg Louganis and be the best me I can be.

Afterword

Andy went to Deephaven School for grades 1-4, and when he was about to leave he sent me a letter. He wrote, "I've learned math and spelling and I had fun for four years. Thanks for being a good teacher and a good secretary." (I had acted as a secretrary in helping with this book.)

Andy is now in 7th grade in Minnetonka. He still has to work a little harder in written language and in math, but he enjoys school and is doing well. He likes to work on his difficult subjects in a small group setting. Andy sent two letters to Greg Louganis and a copy of the book, but he has not yet received a reply.

Andy's present hobbies are basketball, soccer, bicycling, drawing, and playing Nintendo. His parents believe that this book will always remind him there are no limits to what he can achieve.

Matt Patterson

Matt Patterson is a fine example of how an early bad break can be overcome with determination. Matt was born five weeks prematurely and didn't get enough oxygen at birth. This set him back in muscle strength, balance, and coordination, and made handwriting and gym especially difficult for him. In addition, organizing his work was a challenge.

Matt decided to tackle his problem with handwriting by learning to type on a computer. By the time he wrote his chapter for this book in 4th grade he could type 31 words per minute! He also had a positive attitude, so with Matt a little encouragement went a long way.

His love of sports, especially baseball, kept Matt physically active, and he was becoming a pretty good athlete. **Matt** knew Don **Matt**ingly from his extensive baseball card collection, and added him to my list of famous left-handers.

I decided to write about Don Mattingly who is famous as a baseball player because he won 3 GOLD GLOVE AWARDS,

Don Mattingly

by Matt Patterson, age 10 years, 3 months

I decided to write about Don Mattingly who is famous as a baseball player because he won 3 Gold Glove Awards, was the 1985 M.V.P., and the Batting Champion in 1984.

He was born on April 20, 1961, in Evansville, Indiana. His parents named him Donald Arthur Mattingly. His father was a railroad postal worker, his mother was a housewife. He was the youngest of 5 children.

In school he was ambidextrous, using his right and left hands. When he was three, a neighbor gave him a Yankees cap and he wanted to play for the Yankees. At 7 he was the best pitcher in Little League. When he was 9, Don played on a team for 12 year olds and was the M.V.P.

At age 18 he married Kim Sexton, who was still in high school. They lived with his in-laws. His wife was a cashier during the off season. In 1979 they had a son named Taylor Patrick.

When Mattingly was a teenager he was scouted by several teams. In June 1979 he was the 490th draft choice. He thought about going to college but decided to accept the Yankees' $20,000 bonus for signing with them to play in the minor leagues.

In 1981 St. Louis Cardinals outfielder Willie McGee, who played in Nashville that season, said, "I thought he was one of the best left-handed hitters I have ever seen. Even then he was something special."

Don Mattingly is the most consistent player in the A.L. In the last 4 years he had more than 100 RBIs. In 2 of the 4 years he had 200 or more hits, and for 3 of the 4 years he led the American League in doubles.

In 1984, after his first full season in the major leagues, he earned an A.L. batting title. He was picked as the league's M.V.P. in 1985. By the end of 1987 he had hit more than thirty home runs in three straight seasons, becoming the first Yankee to do so since Mickey Mantle and Roger Maris.

Don Mattingly is one of the best players in baseball. He still plays first base for the Yankees. I really don't usually like to write stories, but writing about Don Mattingly I liked!

Afterword

Matt is now in the 8th grade and still enjoys baseball. Other hobbies are basketball, building models, drawing, and video games. His interest in baseball cards grew after he wrote his chapter for this book.

After sending off a letter and a copy of the earlier version of this book to Don Mattingly, Matt received an autographed photo of his hero. Matt continues to follow Don Mattingly's career through sports reports on television and in the newspaper.

His parents tell me that Matt is doing well in school and that his confidence in himself has steadily grown. They write that "It is hard to remember that the six-foot teenager on the basketball team once found it difficult to bounce a ball or run in kindergarten." Matt has truly come a long way.

Kirk Miller

Kirk Miller was in 4th grade when he wrote his chapter about Tom Cruise. A warm and friendly person, Kirk expressed himself very well in words, but had to concentrate on not letting his talkative nature get him into trouble. He also had to work hard at not being too competitive, since it's important for all of us to be good losers as well as good winners.

Kirk was a good reader and was capable of handling his school responsibilities well when he made his best effort. I remember him as very outgoing, an excellent athlete, and very popular among his classmates. He had many leadership qualities, and while he was at Deephaven he made steady progress in learning how to use them in a positive way.

While researching this chapter, Kirk made a trip to London and brought back a magazine about Tom Cruise.

I wanted to write about Tom Cruise who is famous as a movie star because I like his movies. He was born on July 3, 1962 in Syracuse, New York.

Tom Cruise

by Kirk Miller, age 10 years, 2 months

I wanted to write about Tom Cruise who is famous as a movie star because I like his movies. He was born on July 3, 1962, in Syracruse, New York. His name then was Thomas Cruise Mopother IV. His parents were an electrical engineer and a teacher. They were poor. He had three sisters who had learning problems.

He went to eight grade schools and three high schools. He knew that he had a reading problem. When he was eight years old he had to have special reading classes. To try and prove himself he took part in a lot of sports.

After high school, Tom Cruise worked in New York City as a busboy and took acting lessons. After a few months Cruise got a minor film role in the movie *Endless Love*. In 1981 he got a part in the movie *Taps*. In 1983 he was in four movies: *Tijuana* or *Losin' It*, *Risky Business*, *All the Right Moves*, and *The Outsiders*. Cruise acted in *Legend* in 1985, and in 1986 he was in *Top Gun* and *The Color of Money*.

Tom Cruise suffered from dyslexia and had a hard time learning to read. Now he reads all his scripts himself.

At age 25 he married Mimi Rogers, who was an actress. Tom feels it is very helpful to be married to an actress. Tom has no children yet.

Tom Cruise wants to do more acting, car racing, and to have "a lot of kids." His idea for his next movie is to be in a car racing film.

It was fun to learn about Tom Cruise.

Afterword

Kirk Miller is now in 8th grade and is doing very well in school. In fact, his parents tell me that he made his school's honor roll the last two years! He is still very active and outgoing, and two of his big interests right now are soccer and rollerblading.

After we produced the first version of this book, Kirk sent a copy of it with a letter to Tom Cruise. He is still hoping for a reply. Tom Cruise's movie about car racing, called *Days of Thunder,* has come out since then.

I should mention that Kirk was one of the students who was not in my classroom every day or even every week. He came in only when he needed a little extra help, but he wanted to be involved with this book enough to devote some extra time and effort to researching and writing his chapter. His parents feel that the experience had a positive effect on his life that is still with him today.

Margo Holen Dinneen

In addition to being the driving force behind both editions of *If They Can Do It, We Can Too!*, Margo Holen Dinneen was a committed advocate for her students as she coordinated this Deaconess Press publication.

Mrs. Dinneen remains in contact with a number of the students whose work appears in this book, and she continues to teach children with special needs at Deephaven Elementary School. She lives in Minnetonka, Minnesota with her husband.

Brad Sampson

Matt Patterson

Andrew Kroese

P.J. Berntl

Jaime Keefer

Elizabeth Nelson

Andy Wrase

Aubrey Rahn

Tom Rawitzer

Peter Richter

Chris Bloomer

Shawn SVOboda

Will Martin

#20 Kenny Allen

Jesse Richter

Kirk Miller

Tracy Fuller

Matthew Kroese

A Parent's Perspective
by Susan Kroese

Our sons will soon be twelve years old. As I thought about how I would write the story of the last six years, I experienced the powerful emotions of that period all over again. But while our L.D. story has its share of sadness and frustration, it is also a story of love, hope, and success.

Andrew and Matthew were born prematurely, with extremely low birth weights. Although they had no health problems, our first year was full of concerns about their growth and development.

Over the next few years, their development seemed normal; we experienced the joys and worries that anyone with toddlers has. As parents of active twins, you live from moment to moment, and are relieved just to get through the day with no accidents or injuries.

We had been told that learning differences were common in children born prematurely. It was evident the boys were lagging behind other children their age, but we were certain they would catch up by the time they entered school. Our sons were happy and well adjusted, so I tried not to worry about the possibility of learning differences.

About midway through kindergarten, Andrew and Matthew started to have trouble in school. They didn't tell us about it, but we sensed it from the excuses they would come up with for not being able to go to school. I encouraged them to talk, but got nowhere. The frustration was building for all of us.

Then one day after school, Andrew broke down sobbing, telling me he didn't understand the teacher and couldn't follow what was going on in class. Matthew was having the same problems, but was less emotional about it. I consoled them as best I could, but after they had gone to bed, I broke down, too! I thought we had done all we could to see that they were ready for school, and now it seemed like my worst fears had become reality.

We met with their teachers, and while they were concerned about them, they wanted Andrew and Matthew to get through kindergarten before making any final judgments. The rest of the year was awful; Andrew and Matthew became increasingly unhappy, and I became more afraid.

Making things worse was the fact that two families we knew who had had premature babies at the same time Andrew and Matthew were born were already identifying their children's learning progress as accelerated! Although it isn't helpful or fair to make comparisons between your own children and others, it is an all too common response. I wondered what could have happened to my sons.

In spite of our trepidation, Andrew and Matthew entered first grade. When it eventually became clear that they were having an even more difficult time than they did in kindergarten, they were tested and found to be experiencing some forms of learning differences. At the end of the school year they were not ready to move on. So their friends went off to second grade, making Andrew and Matthew the oldest students in their class.

In spite of the fact that we were getting tremendous help and support from our school, family, and friends, I couldn't forget what it was like for "slow" kids when I was growing up. They were labelled not only by classmates, but also by teachers. They were the kids that at most would just "get by." And as I've mentioned, it is almost impossible not to notice the achievements of your child's peers; I was aware that some of our friends and relatives had exceptionally bright children who were reading fourth grade books in second grade, while we were still struggling through first grade readers. At that time I couldn't sit down with my sons and help them with their reading, because I knew I would end up crying. I felt so sorry for them, and for us. I didn't want them to be seen as stupid or be made fun of. I wanted to protect them from all the hurt I feared would come.

Looking back, I can see that I was letting my emotions and anxieties get out of control. For during the two years I spent wringing my hands, our school was doing an incredible job of teaching Andrew and Matthew. Although we were in close contact with the school all along, I was only hearing the negatives in each conference. Once I decided to recognize the positives and really listen to the teachers and to my sons, I realized they were okay. They didn't like the fact they were held back, or that they weren't in the top reading groups, but they were enjoying other successes in class. I asked for more information from the school, and the teachers showed me how I could be more effective in helping Andrew and Matthew learn. I finally felt like I was becoming part of the solution for them, and not part of the problem.

Our two kids have gotten wonderful attention and encouragement over the last five years. Not only have we had dedicated and involved teachers all along, but our family and friends have also been there to support us and the boys. Of course, much of the credit for their achievements goes to Andrew and Matthew themselves. They have been committed to trying their best, and at times have actually offered encouragement and support to me and my husband. Andrew and Matthew are perceptive, creative, healthy, and happy kids with great self-esteem. What more could a parent hope for?

I realize that there may be new challenges and frustrations for our sons as they go through school, but they understand their learning difference and know how hard they will have to work. They also know they'll always have our support.

What we find most encouraging is the increased awareness of learning differences in schools and in society; for instance, now there are colleges with L.D. programs. As we observe these changes, we know that our sons' options in life won't be limited.

This story wouldn't be complete without my giving thanks to one very special L.D. teacher, Margo Holen Dinneen. She gives her students more love, attention, and encouragement than a parent could ever hope for. You will be very lucky if you find a Margo in your child's future. Whatever Andrew and Matthew do when they grow up will truly be a tribute to her hard work.

In closing, the best advice I can pass on to parents of L.D. children is to listen and talk to your sons and daughters. Don't deny the problems, but instead talk openly about both the negatives and positives of their situations. And remember never to let your hopes for your children diminish; as I now know, we all learn in different ways!